WHERE WE GATHER

WE GATHER AT A CHRISTIAN CHURCH

A Place in Our Community

by Lisa J. Amstutz

PEBBLE
a capstone imprint

Published by Pebble, an imprint of Capstone
1710 Roe Crest Drive, North Mankato, Minnesota 56003
capstonepub.com

Library of Congress Cataloging-in-Publication Data is available on the Library of Congress website.
ISBN: 9798875223006 (hardcover)
ISBN: 9798875222955 (paperback)
ISBN: 9798875222962 (ebook PDF)

Summary: Churches are community gathering places. People come to pray and celebrate together. Learn what's inside, who gathers there, and what makes the space unique.

Editorial Credits
Designer: Sarah Bennett; Media Researchers: Jo Miller and Svetlana Zhurkin; Production Specialist: Tori Abraham

Image Credits
Getty Images: FatCamera, 14, Jose Luis Pelaez Inc, 15, kali9, 17, SDI Productions, 18, SolStock, 19; Shutterstock: Duc Huy Nguyen, 8, Joanna Dorota, 21, Juicy FOTO, 7, Junior Braz, 12, Katarzyna Wierzba, 9, kizuuuneko, design element (throughout), Leena Robinson, cover, Matyas Rehak, 6, Nagel Photography, 10, Pvince73, 4, Satit Soithongcharoen, 13, shulers, 16, trabantos, 5, U. J. Alexander, 11

Printed and bound in China. 6274

Table of Contents

Words in **bold** are in the glossary.

What Is a Church?

A church is a place where people gather. They sing and make music. They pray and worship. The pastor or another church leader shares a lesson about God. People at a church are called Christians.

There are millions of churches around the world.

A church in Sweden

Some churches have a tall **steeple**. Bells inside chime. Churches come in many shapes and sizes. A church can be big and grand or small and simple.

Who Worships Here?

People of all ages gather in churches to worship. Some churches have only a few members. Some have thousands. Inside each church is a place to gather everyone together.

Some churches are one-room buildings.

People go to church to worship God. They follow the teachings of Jesus Christ. The Bible is their holy book.

Christians follow the teachings of the Holy Bible.

Come Inside!

Many churches have long benches inside called **pews**. People sit close together. Some churches have rows of chairs instead.

Some churches have high ceilings. They keep the room cool.

Pastors and some other church leaders are called clergy members.

At the front is a stage. The speaker stands at a **pulpit**. Behind it is the **altar**. It is often rectangular. It is where bread and wine are blessed.

Crucifixes are symbols of Jesus Christ and Christianity.

The symbol of Christianity is a cross. A big cross on the outside of the building tells people it is a church. Inside, there are more crosses. Some may have the figure of Jesus on them. These are called crucifixes.

Some churches have a stone **font**. It holds holy water. People dip their fingers in it when they enter. They make the sign of the cross with their hands.

Holy water

Some churches have an **organ** with large pipes. Churches may have a piano, drums, or guitars. Tall ceilings help sound carry.

Music is an important part of worship.

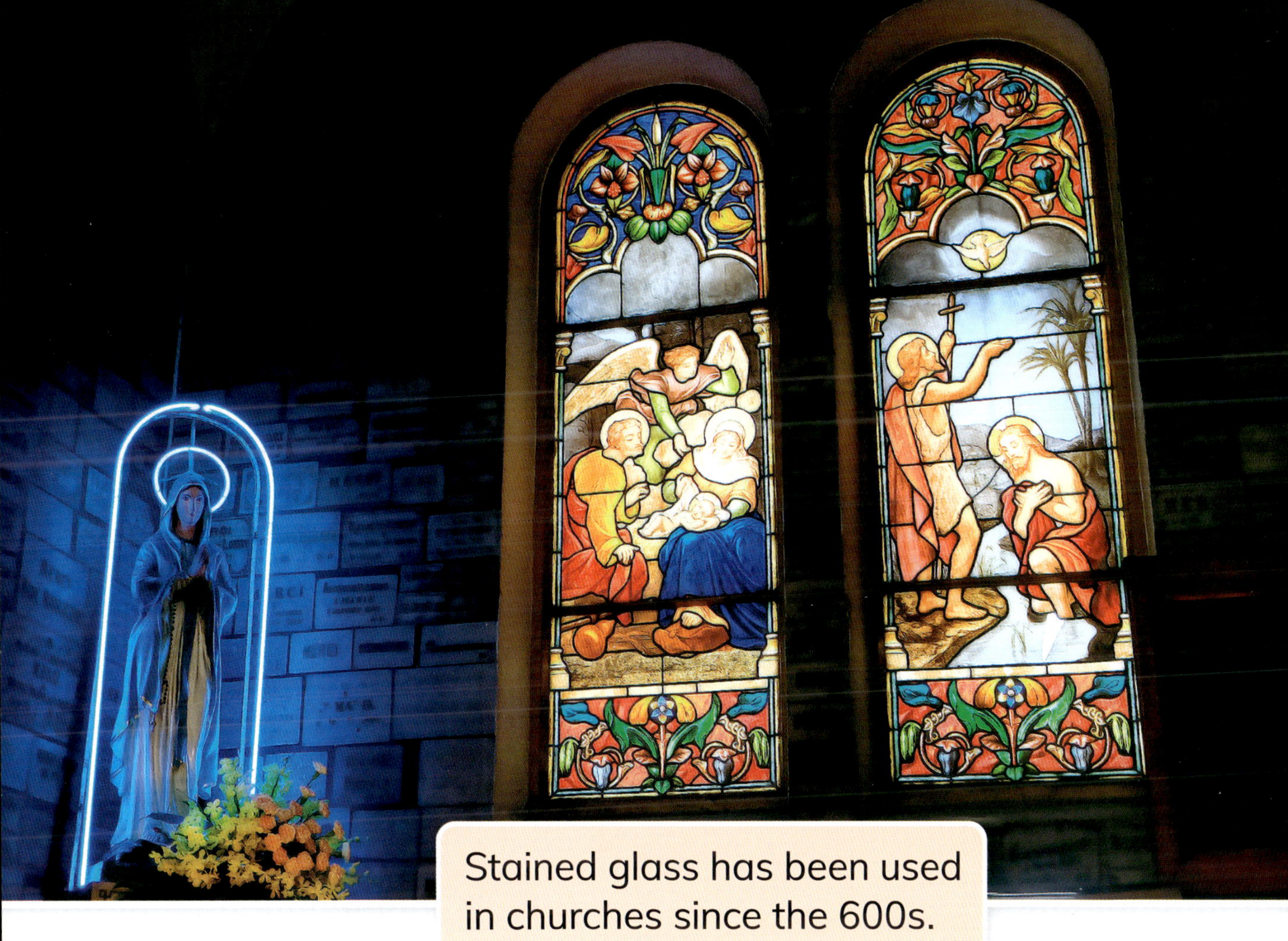

Stained glass has been used in churches since the 600s.

Light shines through windows. They often are made of colorful stained glass. They may show stories from the Bible. Churches might have statues or paintings too.

A church has rooms for people to meet. Adults and kids have classes. They study and discuss the Bible. Other groups may meet there too.

People often wear nice clothes to church.

Community kitchens make sure everyone has a hot meal.

Many churches have kitchens. Groups cook meals for special events or to feed the hungry. Family and friends can dine together at big tables. Sometimes everyone brings a dish to share. This is called a potluck.

Reaching Out

Churches host events, such as weddings or holiday meals. They have bake sales or dinners to raise money for groups or organizations. People from the community come.

Many weddings take place at churches.

Churches do other fun things too. Some have **festivals** and parades. Music programs bring singers and other musicians together. Other churches have sports teams.

Church choirs bring people together to sing as a group.

People at churches try to help others in need. They may offer food, clothing, or shelter. They might help people find a new place to live.

Some churches have free meals every day. Others give out groceries or supplies.

Churches offer places for different groups to meet.

Life can be hard. Meeting with others who struggle can help. Groups may meet at a church to talk and support one another. Churches are a place for everyone to gather and learn together.

Draw a Community Church

The next time you walk or drive around your neighborhood, take a look around. Keep track of how many churches you pass. What do they look like? Are there interesting features that you like?

Draw a picture of a church. What does it look like? Does it have a dome or steeple? Does it have stained glass windows? Are there crosses?

Glossary

altar (ALL-tuhr)—a table or box where special items are set

festival (FES-tuh-vuhl)—a holiday or celebration

font (FAWNT)—a container of holy water

organ (OR-guhn)—a keyboard instrument with a large set of pipes that carry sound

pew (PEW)—a long bench found in a church

pulpit (PUHL-pit)—a platform where a preacher speaks

steeple (STEE-puhl)—a church tower

Read More

Andrews, Elizabeth. *Christianity*. Minneapolis: DiscoverRoo, an imprint of Pop!, 2024.

Bolte, Mari. *Christian Festivals and Traditions*. North Mankato, MN: Pebble, an imprint of Capstone, 2025.

Cunningham, Sarah Raymond. *This Is the Church*. Minneapolis: Beaming Books, 2020.

Internet Sites

BBC: Religious Education
bbc.co.uk/bitesize/subjects/zxnygk7

Kiddle: Christianity Facts for Kids
kids.kiddle.co/Christianity

National Geographic: Christianity 101
education.nationalgeographic.org/resource/christianity-101

Index

About the Author

Lisa J. Amstutz is the author of more than 150 children's books on topics ranging from applesauce to zebra mussels. An ecologist by training, she enjoys sharing her love of nature with kids. Lisa lives on a small farm with her family.